Outdoor Survival

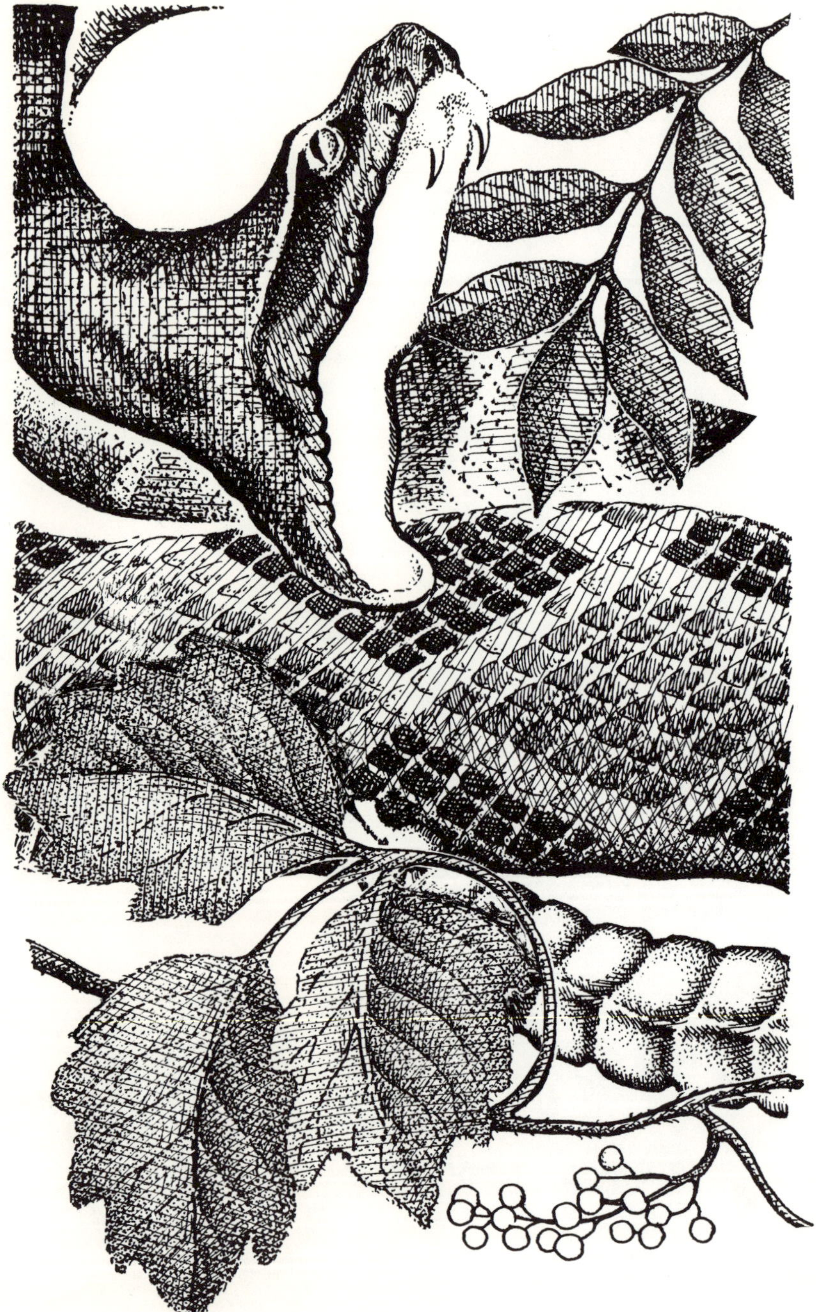

Outdoor Survival

BY CHARLES PLATT
Illustrated by Rod Slater

A Concise Guide

FRANKLIN WATTS | NEW YORK | LONDON | 1976

J613.69
Plat

Library of Congress Cataloging in Publication Data

Platt, Charles, 1949–
    Outdoor survival.

    Includes index.
    SUMMARY: Brief hints on how to avoid outdoor emergencies accompany discussions of what to do if faced with a survival situation.
    1. Wilderness survival—Juvenile literature. 2. Hiking—Juvenile literature. [1. Survival. 2. Hiking] I. Slater, Rod. II. Title.
GV200.5.P42   613.6′9   75-35883
ISBN 0–531–01128–3

Copyright © 1976 by Franklin Watts, Inc.
All rights reserved
Printed in the United States of America
5 4 3 2 1

Contents

Introduction   1

START OUT WELL PREPARED   3
Could It Happen to You?   3
Know Your Limits   5
Planning Ahead   5
Anticipating the Weather   7

COPING WITH AN EMERGENCY   10
The Problem of Panic   10
Shock   11
Exposure   11
Other Cold Hazards   12
Heat Hazards   13
Other Emergencies   14

FIRE AND WATER   23
No Matches?   23
Building the Fire   24
Putting It Out   25
Is It Safe to Drink?   25
Water Out of Thin Air   28
Water in the Desert   28
Water at Sea   30
Water Substitutes   32

FINDING FOOD   33
What Do You Need?   33

Is it Poisonous? 33
Some Safe Bets 34
If You're Desperate... 36
Where to Look 36
Eating Animals 37
Cook It First 39

FINDING YOUR WAY 40

Set Out or Stay Put? 40
Keeping Track 41
Directional Aids 42
The Compass 45
Points to Remember 47

**STAYING PUT
AND SIGNALING 49**

Fires 50
Symbols and Signals 50
Mirror Signaling 51
Maintaining Morale 53

**APPENDIX 1:
YOUR SURVIVAL KIT 55**

**APPENDIX 2:
SOURCES OF SUPPLY 58**

Index 59

**To Simon,
Who Knows How
to Survive**

Outdoor Survival

Introduction

Modern civilization looks after us and takes care of us. When the weather is too wet, too cold, or too hot, our homes protect us from it. When we are hungry there is always food at the local store, and drinking water is as far away as the nearest faucet. In an emergency, help is a phone call away—to the nearest hospital, fire or police department.

It is quite natural to take these services for granted and forget how it would feel without them—how harsh the weather sometimes really is, how much our lives depend on regular meals and drinking water, and how helpless most of us would be in trying to deal with medical emergencies unaided. Why worry about such things when it is so unlikely that we will have to face them?

This attitude is all right at home, but when we take it with us into undeveloped or wilderness areas, it can lead to trouble. Millions of people visit our national parks and forests each year, where frequent roadside services and ranger patrols minimize the chances of an emergency. But every year there are people who *do* run into trouble, whether they are casual tourists whose automobile fails while they are exploring a little-used back road, or hikers who overestimate their strength and underestimate the terrain and the weather. Even a vacationer experienced in the outdoors can make a simple error of judgment that leads without warning to a survival situation: a sprained ankle, a serious fall, a snakebite, or simply getting lost and realizing that a cold night is coming, the sky is filled with storm clouds, and there is nowhere nearby to take shelter.

When you run into trouble of this kind you suddenly realize now helpless you are. It can be very frightening, discovering yourself in real danger, without the protections of civilized life that we normally take for granted.

Fear leads to panic, which interferes with common sense and makes things even worse. It is the aim of this guide to provide background knowledge and practical advice so that if you are ever in a survival situation yourself, you will know what to do. And, even more important, you will know how to reduce the chance of an emergency ever happening to you in the first place.

Start Out Well Prepared

COULD IT HAPPEN TO YOU?

A young friend of mine was visiting friends who had a house in the country. The land behind the house sloped up gradually until it became a high, steep hill with craggy rocks at the summit; his friends had told him that it was an easy afternoon's walk to the top and down again.

His friends were used to being outdoors and seemed to think he was "soft" and lacked stamina, so naturally he wanted to prove them wrong. On the first day of his vacation, while they drove off to a town ten miles away to do some shopping, he decided there and then that he would go out and climb that hill. It looked easy enough. He reckoned to be up it and back by the time his friends returned home.

Soon after he started out, he found that the top of the climb seemed to be retreating. In the clear air the summit looked close; actually, it was not. Still, he was determined not to turn back—even when he noticed storm clouds collecting in the East and heading his way.

Two hours later he was near the top but hardly cared any more. His feet hurt, he was out of breath and aching, and he had to sit down and rest. The clouds had come closer and actually began settling over him, like heavy fog.

With a shock he realized he could no longer see all the way back down. His summer clothing was no protection against the ice-cold mist that quickly seeped through to his skin. He tried to follow the slope of the land but found himself descending the hill on the wrong side, where a steep rock slope blocked his way completely.

He wandered around, shivering and hungry, but could not locate the right path. Darkness was closing in, and with no food, protective clothing, compass, or matches, he might not survive a cold night—even though he was a mere six miles from his starting point.

He was lucky, as it happened. A break in the clouds let him get his bearings, and he was able to avoid losing his way again for long enough to walk down out from under the clouds, to a point where he could manage the rest of the descent even though the sun had set. But in a similar situation you might not be so lucky. It is worth listing the mistakes my friend made so that you can avoid making them yourself.

1. He wore light summer clothing. In mountainous regions the weather changes fast, and evenings are cold. Weather shifts quickly from sun to rain. Always wear or carry extra clothing for protection.

2. He did not carry a compass or matches—always carry both.

3. He underestimated the distance. This is a common error that can be very dangerous. If possible, consult a map before setting out on a long walk. And remember that what an experienced hiker casually calls an "easy afternoon's walk" can be a hard day's work for you.

4. He went off on his own, telling no one where he had gone. Always leave word, or a note, so that in an emergency people will know where to look for you.

5. He ignored danger signals. Despite realizing he had underestimated the distance, and despite the worsening weather, he went on anyway. Always be ready to acknowledge warning signs and change your plans accordingly; don't press on regardless.

6. He set out in shoes made for city use and discovered how easy it is to develop blisters—and how painful blisters can be. Wear proper climbing shoes when hiking. Besides being fully waterproof, they are pliable, soft, and their soles grip well.

7. Most important: By climbing the hill, he was trying to prove something to his friends and to himself. This attitude led to many of his mistakes and is the cause of countless emergency situations every year. The outdoors is there to be enjoyed, not to be conquered.

KNOW YOUR LIMITS

This is the first rule. Exhilarated by being outdoors, it is easy to overestimate your strength, have fantasies about being a mountaineer, set yourself unrealistic goals, and try to prove you can achieve them, meanwhile ignoring the weather, the time, and your own inexperience.

You will probably enjoy things more if you take a different attitude. Be honest about evaluating your own strengths and weaknesses. Increase your skill and stamina by degrees rather than in an all-out onslaught. Once you understand your own limits, stay within them until you are really at home outdoors. Most important, never accept a dare, or try to prove you are more experienced and capable than you really are.

PLANNING AHEAD

Knowing your limits is one important way to avoid emergency situations. Planning ahead is equally important. Whether you are contemplating a two-week vacation or an afternoon's walk such as the one that my unfortunate friend decided to take, you'll be less likely to run into difficulties if you plan your excursion rather than set off on impulse.

If you are planning to visit an area that you know nothing about, write to the local chamber of commerce or tourist office asking for free literature describing their part of the world. Even better, you can obtain large-scale maps of the terrain in the U.S.A. and Canada, ideal for use when out walking. They show all the important features of the landscape and the contours of the ground. For areas east of the Mississippi, write to the U.S.

Geological Survey, Washington, D.C. 20242. For areas west of the Mississippi, write to the U.S. Geological Survey, Federal Center, Denver, CO 80225. For Canada, write to the Map Distribution Office, Survey and Mapping Branch, Department of Energy, Mines and Resources, Ottawa, Ontario, Canada. First ask for an index map of the general area; once you have this you can narrow your focus to areas covered by individual sheets of the large-scale maps. Allow a few weeks for your order to be processed.

Another important aspect of being well prepared is being well equipped. The most important item of equipment is a survival kit; you can buy these ready-made at camping supply stores, or you can assemble your own, but some kind of kit, containing items useful in an emergency, should always be carried. We describe a possible kit in some detail in Appendix 1; a smaller version to be carried on short trips should include the following:

- Matches (in a waterproof container that will not break if stepped on or fallen on)
- Knife (sheath type in a leather case)
- Compass (see the chapter "Finding Your Way")
- Small first-aid kit (Band-Aids, bandages, antiseptic, aspirin)
- Snakebite kit (available from camping goods suppliers)
- Nylon lightweight cord
- Whistle
- Flashlight
- Metal mirror (see the chapter "Staying Put and Signaling")
- Paper and pencil
- Water purifying tablets (from a drugstore)
- Fishing line and hooks
- Space blanket

On a short, casual walk you can prune down the number of items still further, but we suggest you always include matches, knife, compass, flashlight, and "space" blanket. The latter is a sheet of silvered plastic, about four feet by eight, so thin that it folds into a pocket-size square weighing a couple of ounces. If you are ever stranded you can wrap yourself in it and it will retain 90 percent of your body heat. It is also useful for collecting drinking water (see the chapter "Fire and Water").

Sunglasses and a water flask are other desirable items to have along.

Where clothing is concerned, naturally you should be prepared for the weather conditions of the time of year. In summer this does *not* mean short-sleeved shirts—unless you are immune to sunburn! Your pack should include something to cover your head and the back of your neck on long walks. In winter, pay particular attention to protecting your feet, hands, and face from frostbite—more on this in the next chapter.

Lastly, get a tetanus booster shot from your doctor. Tetanus (lockjaw) sometimes results from wounds made by rusty or dirty objects. It is well worth immunizing yourself.

ANTICIPATING THE WEATHER

Foul weather, at best, is a disappointment. If you are trapped in it, it is uncomfortable; if you are unprepared for it, it can be dangerous. The temperature does not have to be below freezing in order to freeze to death. If your clothes are soaked through and there is a strong wind, just a few hours of exposure, without shelter, can be dangerous at temperatures below 40 degrees. Rain is your enemy; learn how to predict when it's on the way.

Not all clouds are danger signals. A *cumulus* is a white, puffy blob of cloud. When many cumuli are scattered in a blue sky the weather will almost certainly be dry. On the other hand, if you see a cumulus cloud growing bigger, into a towering heap that is gray at the bottom, beware—this is a *cumulonimbus* (a thunderhead), bringing heavy rain, lightning, and

CUMULUS

NIMBOSTRATUS

CIRRUS

sometimes hail. If you have to take shelter, choose a small evergreen tree rather than a tall pine to minimize the danger from lightning. For the same reason, avoid sheltering in a shed or tent isolated in the middle of a flat, open space.

Nimbostratus, a heavy, low cloud layer that often stretches in furrows across the sky, foretells a heavy rainstorm within four hours.

A *cirrus* is a high, thin, white wisp of cloud, like a horse's tail. Seen in the morning in a bright blue sky, cirri should fade away during the day. In a grayish sky, they are likely to thicken, becoming *cirrostratus*—a high blanket of white veins that produces a halo effect around sun or moon. Similar but with less texture, *altostratus,* looking like an undefined gray or dull blue haze, reduces the sun to a vague blob of light. Both cirrostratus and altostratus herald rain.

After a storm you may see *cirrocumuli,* high clouds textured like fish scales. They are thin, allow sunlight to filter through quite strongly, and usually fade away.

A lot of dew or frost on the ground in the morning is a good sign (water on the ground suggests there will be less in the air), and the old rhyme

> Red sky in the morning
> Sailors take warning
> Red sky at night
> Sailors' delight

does often hold true, especially in coastal regions.

"Uncertain" winds—strong gusts from different directions—indicate uncertain weather; and a steady west wind (*from* the west) usually means fine weather.

Lastly, to check the temperature without a thermometer: If crickets are chirping, count the number of chirps in fifteen seconds, add 40—the approximate temperature in degrees Fahrenheit!

Coping with an Emergency

Being well prepared and using common sense in the outdoors will reduce the chances of your getting into difficulties. But even the most careful person will occasionally run into some kind of trouble. When the worst does happen, what do you do?

THE PROBLEM OF PANIC

"Don't panic" is easy advice to give but hard advice to follow. Most people tend to act wildly without thinking when they are scared, even though they really may know quite well the sensible thing to do. For example, the camper who crawls out of his tent and finds himself face to face with a bear may know that the correct thing to do is freeze, because sudden movements may scare or provoke the animal. In actuality, however, your first impulse will be to get up and run; if you give in to this impulse, you may well fall and hurt yourself even if you escape attack.

It takes a conscious effort to control panic. If possible, force yourself to pause, sit down, look around, breathe slowly, and assess the situation before doing anything. If you have to take immediate action to save your skin, you should still try to do something to gain more time in which to think. If possible, avoid committing yourself to any one course of action until you are certain it is the right course.

If you have a companion, you can rely on one another and keep up morale by discussing the situation. If you are alone, it is much harder—you have only yourself to turn to. It may help to do something that seems a little bit crazy—like hugging your backpack and shutting your eyes, or talking to yourself. Do whatever will make you feel calmer. Remember that the situation you are in, whatever it is, is not unique; hundreds or thousands of other people have been in a similar predicament and have come through it one way or another. Itemize your resources, avoid wild fantasies about the worst that could happen, work out a plan of action, and, in addition, work out a contingency plan to be used in case anything interferes with your first plan.

Controlling panic is never easy; but if you can just make yourself pause, sit, and think, the battle is at least half won.

SHOCK

Any emergency can give you a shock, or surprise. But when we talk about shock, here, we mean a particular physical reaction that usually happens to someone who is injured. A person in shock will be pale, trembling, sweating (though with cool skin), thirsty, and the pulse will be fast. The more serious the injury, the worse the shock condition. It should be taken seriously. Ignoring it and pressing on regardless is not a good idea. The treatment, if possible, is complete rest, for a full day, and warmth. The shock victim should lie down with the feet higher than the head, beside a fire, out of the wind, and as relaxed as possible. The victim should be kept warm, but not so warm as to cause sweating.

EXPOSURE

The effects of exposure may sometimes be confused with the symptoms of shock. When we say someone is suffering from exposure, it generally means he or she has been exposed to low temperatures long enough to reduce the body's own temperature. Technically, this is known as *hypothermia*. The body burns food to maintain its temperature; when your energy reserves run low, or when cold air is taking away the body's heat faster than the body can generate more, a reduction in body temperature will eventually result.

As with shock, the victim will be pale and trembling. However, there will be no sweating and the pulse will be slow, not fast. Look, also, for slow breathing, slurred speech, clumsiness, loss of memory, and dilated pupils.

The treatment, again, is rest and warmth. Hot drinks are especially good for bringing the body's temperature back up to normal. Physical activity—swinging the arms, running up and down, etc.—may make the sufferer feel better for a while but *worse* in the long run, by burning up still more of his diminished energy reserves. Resting beside a fire, under as many dry clothes as possible, is the proper treatment.

Remember that, as we have already mentioned, you don't need freezing temperatures to be frozen to death. If your clothes are wet through to your skin, they no longer work to insulate you from the weather. A temperature of below 40 degrees and a strong wind are enough to cause severe chilling within a few hours and even death. If you find yourself stranded in a rainstorm, and you don't have proper protection from it, it is usually wiser to take shelter and wait for the storm to pass rather than to make a run for it.

OTHER COLD HAZARDS

Bad weather can always make an emergency worse, or it can be an emergency all on its own. Knowing how to make a fire (see next chapter) is your best defense against the hazard of exposure. You should also know how to deal with frostbite, however.

The hands, feet, and face are the parts of the body farthest from the heart. When it is cold, the body tends to reduce the extent to which blood is circulated. With reduced circulation, hands, feet, and face are no longer kept properly warm. Grayish or yellow-white spots form on the skin, where it begins to freeze. You can see it before you begin to feel it. Any area that becomes numb may be affected.

You can avoid frostbite by keeping yourself covered as

much as possible. Making faces, slapping the skin, or chewing gum (with your mouth closed, to keep the cold air out) will also help, by maintaining blood circulation.

If you do suffer frostbite, do *not* rub snow on it. This "remedy" is actually harmful. Frostbitten skin is injured skin. Treat it gently. Put warm garments over it or apply body heat—cup your hand over a frostbitten ear, warm frostbitten fingers under your armpit. At home, apply tepid, body-temperature water. After the skin thaws, do not allow it to become frostbitten again soon afterward; this kills the tissues.

HEAT HAZARDS

Being exposed to too much heat is just as serious as being exposed to too much coldness. Desert areas of America are often as hot as 120 degrees in the shade; without water, your survival time is only a couple of days under these conditions.

Even if you do have water, you will need at least one gallon a day to survive. The body loses enormous amounts of fluid through perspiration and other body wastes, and all of this must be replaced.

If you are ever stranded in extreme heat, do not stay put and wait for rescue unless you are in a region that is frequently patrolled. However, you should wait for night to come before setting out on foot. The desert night may be as much as 50 degrees cooler than the day, allowing you to walk as much as twenty miles—impossible in daytime heat. While waiting for the sun to go down you should try to find some shade, and if possible support yourself—on heaped, loose wood, for example—so that you are a few inches off the ground, which radiates a lot of heat. If possible, sleep. You may try to collect water (as described in the next chapter) but remember that the work of collecting it will make you perspire more than ever, and if you are able to gather only a few pints, this will not be enough to lengthen your survival time appreciably.

If you have food, eat sparingly. Protein actually takes

water from body reserves in the process of digestion. Eat carbohydrates and avoid dried or dehydrated foods.

If you *have* to travel during the day, keep your body loosely covered. Sunburn is a major hazard, even if you already have a deep tan. Light-colored clothing, as most people know, absorbs less heat than dark colors, so white clothing is your best protection.

OTHER EMERGENCIES

Apart from the general tactics that should be followed in cases of shock, exposure, panic, and hot and cold weather, there are specific actions to be taken in specific emergencies such as snakebite, for example.

The following list of emergencies and appropriate action in each case are listed alphabetically, for reference.

Animals
Most North American animals are not dangerous to man, with the exception of grizzly bears, polar bears, and walruses. However, animals that have become familiar with humans (park bears, for instance) and are no longer afraid of us may be very unpredictable. As we mentioned at the beginning of this chapter, the right thing to do is stop moving. Sudden movements may seem like an attack to the animal, in which case it will fight back. If you do nothing, the animal should eventually lose interest.

Contrary to popular opinion, incidentally, wolves are generally not dangerous to man.

Avalanches
Any steep slope that has streaks of gray, loose stone, earth, and dust running down it is a danger zone. If there is snow on the ground, avoid treeless strips running down a hillside and watch for lateral cracks in the snow on any steep slope.

When old frozen snow is covered with new snow, or when the afternoon sun partially melts existing snow, conditions are ideal for avalanches and landslides; proceed carefully. Uprooted trees and vegetation at the bottom of a slope are immediate signs that the area is dangerous; conversely, if the slope is densely covered with trees and vegetation, you can feel fairly secure.

In a landslide, your first action is to try to outrun it. If that is impossible, try to crouch down below a large rock outcropping, with hands behind your neck, hoping the slide will pass over you.

In a snowslide, try to get rid of all impediments such as backpack, skis, or snowshoes. Swim with the slide, keeping your hands near your face to give protection and to prevent suffocation if you are smothered.

Blisters

If you are on foot with a long way to travel, and your survival depends on being able to walk, don't underestimate the seriousness of blisters or the quickness with which they develop. Inspect your feet frequently for red patches that are the beginnings of blisters. Apply Band-Aids to these spots or, if you have no Band-Aids, use anything soft, such as moss or leaves, to protect the skin from being rubbed by your shoe. If you do develop blisters you should *not* burst them wide open; this multiplies the pain and increases the chance of infection. Instead, prick a few tiny holes (with pin or knife point) around the edges of each swelling and very gently ease out the fluid through these pinpricks. Wait for the fluid to evaporate and apply a Band-Aid before you continue walking.

Bugs

Mites and chiggers will burrow into the skin, often around your waist. Touch spots with iodine, oil, or pitch to kill the tiny parasites that cause the irritation.

In areas in and around Montana there are ticks that carry

Rocky Mountain fever; get a spotted fever vaccine to immunize yourself before entering these areas, if you are going to be there for a while. Remove ticks with a drop of iodine, or the tip of a hot stick from a fire, to make them let go. Pulling them off often leaves their heads behind in the skin, later causing infection.

Mosquitoes breed in still water, so be prepared if you camp beside a lake or a river that has areas of slow-running water. Electronic mosquito repellers (little black boxes that broadcast a very high-pitched whine) are not at all effective in this author's experience, and their batteries are worn out after just a couple of nights' use. Bug repellent cream is better. You can slap mud on your face if there is no other form of protection, or sleep with your head covered. Remember also to tuck your pants legs into your socks.

If stung by a bee, try to remove its sting with a knife point (sterilized first in a flame), using it as a lever to dig in gently under the sting and pry it up and out. Lemon juice or vinegar are some help in soothing yellowjacket and wasp stings. Fire ashes mixed with water to make a paste are also soothing. But there is no easy way of really "curing" a sting.

An Unexpected Swim
If you are plunged suddenly and unexpectedly into water, try not to lose whatever possessions you may have with you. Avoiding panic and staying afloat are obviously your first concerns, but later, out of the water, you may be lost without the few vital necessities that were swept away from you or sank while you were in the water.

If you are in a fast current, take a moment to see where the current is sweeping you before trying to fight it. It may lead you naturally to a place where you can scramble out. If you are stranded a long swimming distance from the shore in calm water, you can help yourself stay afloat by making "water wings" out of your trousers. Take them off, knot the bottom of each leg, zip the fly closed, grasp the waistband and swing the pants over and down so that the waist part is open as it hits the water, trapping air inside the garment. Quickly close the waist of the pants. The trapped air will provide buoyancy, giving you time to rest. A tent or sleeping bag can be improvised the same way to trap a pocket of air.

Swimming will be easier if you discard your clothes, but bear in mind that once you are out of the water you may need them desperately to protect yourself from heat or cold. Never get rid of your shoes, unless you are certain that when you reach dry land help will be close at hand.

The breast, back, and side strokes are the least tiring for a long distance, and of course you should pause now and then —floating on your back—to rest.

Falling Through Ice

Even in very cold weather there can be patches of thin ice, where decaying plant matter under the ice has created enough local heat to melt it partially. Stay away from dark patches among lighter-colored ice. They are danger areas. Spring is the most unpredictable time of year, so avoid traveling on ice altogether if possible.

If you feel yourself falling, throw your arms out so that you have a chance of spread-eagling over the hole rather than falling through into icy water. Carry a knife when walking on ice, so that if you do fall in you can use the knife blade like an ice pick, stabbing it into the ice and then pulling on it to haul yourself out.

Once out of the water and on solid ground quickly roll in snow to blot up water from your clothes. The snow acts like a sponge. Brush off any that clings to you, then roll in some more, until as much water as possible has been absorbed. Clothes that are totally saturated are very little use to you as protection from the cold (see the earlier section on exposure), so take them off rather than let the water soak through to the rest of your clothes. Try to get warm with a fire and hot drinks before continuing.

Poisonous Plants

The three most common plants that can cause you trouble are poison ivy, poison oak, and poison sumac. All of them have small white or light grayish-green berries. There is no easy cure for the itching, redness, and blistering that contact with the poison produces, but washing right away with soap is a help.

Juice from the berries is quite dangerous to the eyes, and you should never allow any of the plants to be mixed in with firewood, since the fire turns their sap to vapor that can drift on the wind and settle on you. Study the illustrations of these plants carefully.

Quicksand

There is nothing terrifying or mysterious about it, so ignore the folklore and wild stories about people being "sucked down." Quicksand is very soft, wet mud. If you step into it you will sink slowly, pulled down only by gravity. There should be ample time to assess the situation and take action (but this amount of time will be shortened if you thrash around wildly in a panic). Remove a backpack or any other heavy object that you are carrying and throw it to safety. If you are traveling with a companion, he can haul you out with a rope made from clothes knotted together. If you are alone and are out of reach of firm ground, lie out as flat as possible to spread your weight widely, and then make slow, gentle breaststroke motions. Swimming this way in quicksand does work, though naturally it's horribly messy.

Snakebite

If you are traveling well prepared you will have a snakebite kit with you (see Appendix 1, which lists items in a survival kit), with instructions telling you what to do.

If you are bitten by a poisonous snake and you are not prepared, remain calm and act quickly. (The poison will cause immediate redness and swelling.) Open the wound with a knife,

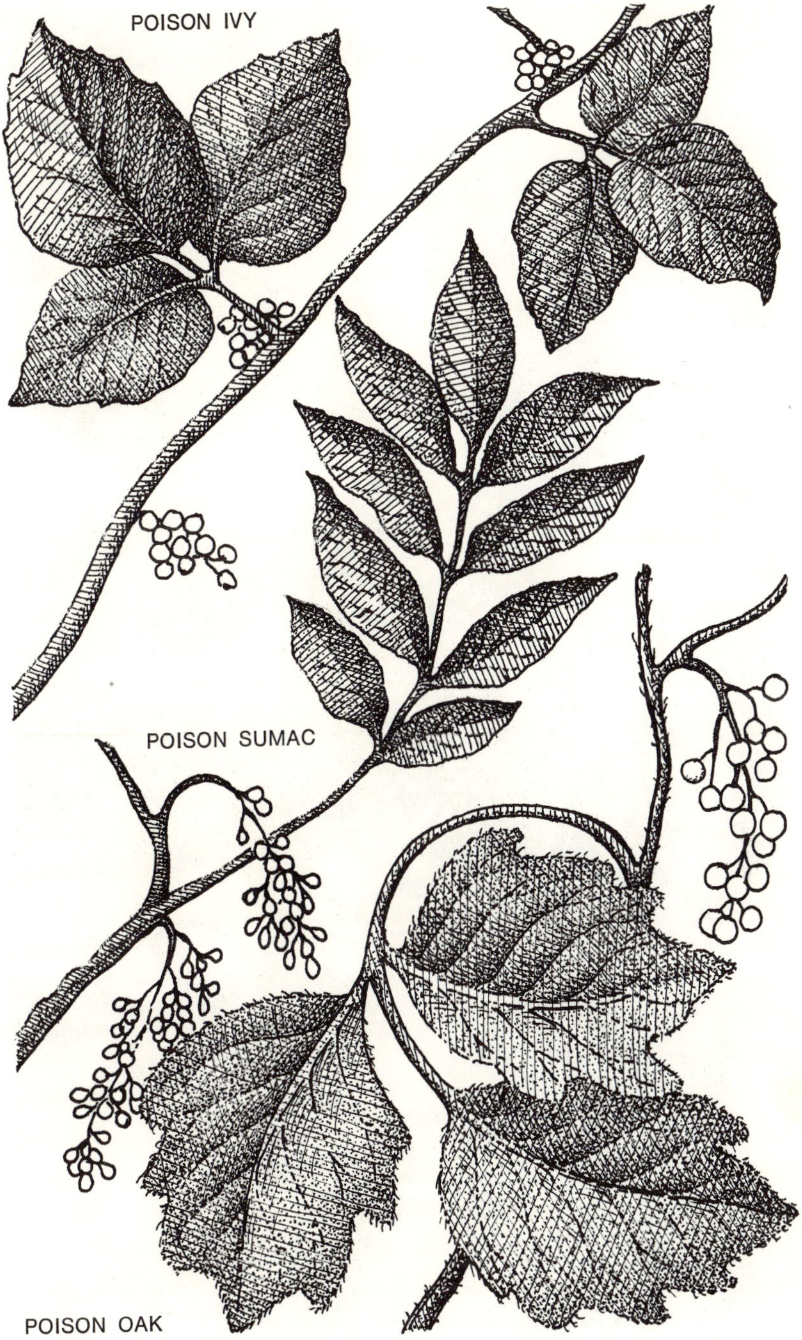
POISON IVY
POISON SUMAC
POISON OAK

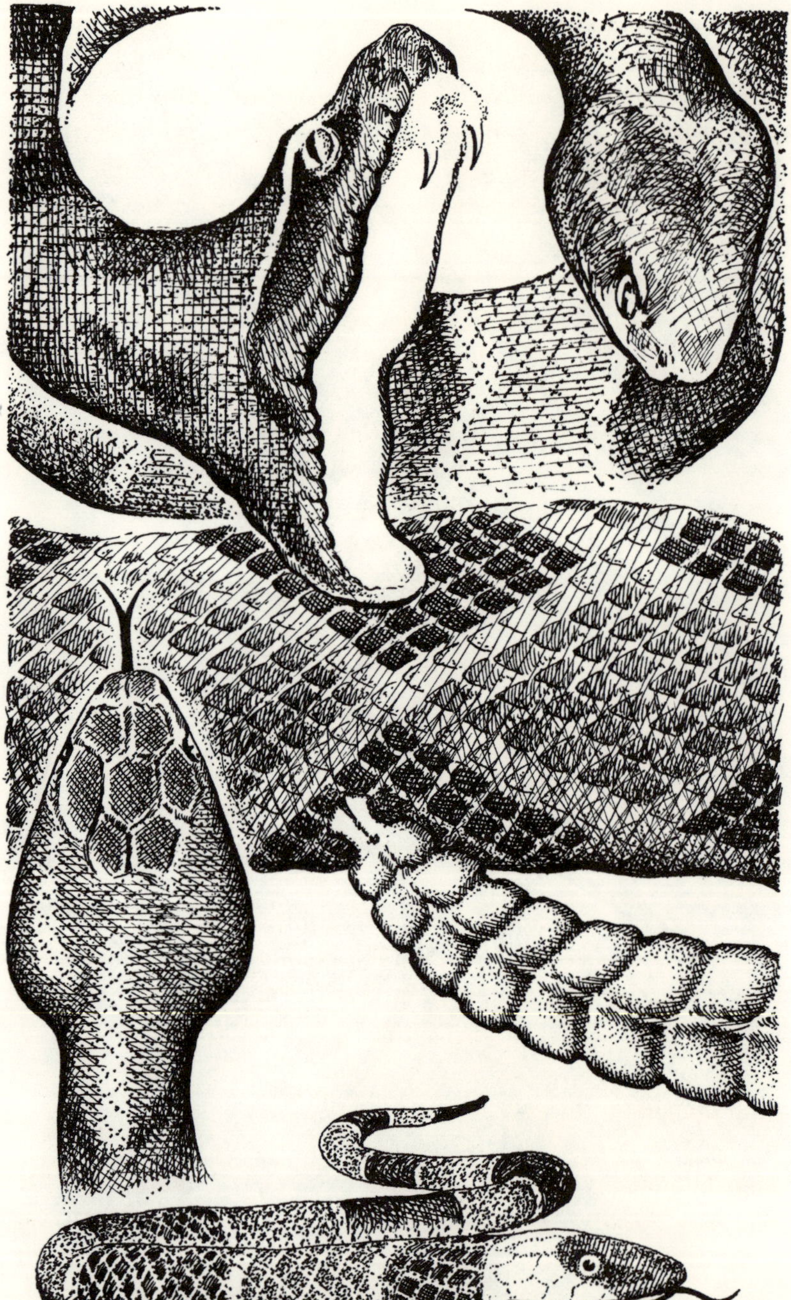

so that it bleeds freely. Then suck out the snake venom (without swallowing it). Use a strip of torn cloth, a piece of string or wire, or a strong vine to make a tourniquet. Loop the tourniquet around the limb, between the bite and your heart, and tighten it as much as possible by pushing a stick through it and turning the stick. Loosen the tourniquet for one minute every half-hour.

Someone should try to kill the snake (with a rock or a club) so that it can be identified when you reach help. If the snake gets away, try to remember exactly what it looked like. There are different antidotes for different kinds of snake venom.

It is very important to lie still and try to remain calm. The more you move or the more you panic, the faster your heart will beat, pumping more of the snake venom through your body. If you are with friends, send someone for help while you lie down. If help is distant, consider whether you can be carried partway there.

Snakebites are less frequent than many people fear. Even if you are bitten, death is very unlikely. In country where there are snakes, avoid walking too quietly, since snakes are most likely to bite when they are surprised. Carry a stick and strike the ground with it as you walk, to let the creatures know that you are there. Also, wear protective boots and sleep off the ground.

If you are faced suddenly with a snake that is poised and ready to strike, freeze. Estimate the distance from the snake to you. It can only strike across a gap that is about two-thirds as long as itself. If there is a larger gap than this, you can immediately retreat. If not, try to summon enough nerve to wait until the *snake* retreats.

Snowblindness
You may not feel snowblindness very much until you rest your eyes indoors or when it gets dark; then, it can be quite unpleasant. Red, burning, watering, and gritty-feeling eyes are

typical. You will also probably have a headache, and it is common to see halos around lights. The treatment is simply resting the eyes in subdued light and taking aspirin. Recovery usually is complete inside of a day, but one attack will make you more vulnerable to future attacks.

Prevent snowblindness by protecting the eyes from glare. If you forgot your sunglasses, improvise—hang fronds, grass, birchbark with a slit cut in it, or a piece of thin fabric over your eyes. And remember, a desert sun is just as treacherous as a snow-country sun.

This section covers the most common hazards and specific kinds of emergencies, where a specific action is needed to save yourself or reduce the effects that you suffer. The next chapter deals with what happens after the original emergency—how to support yourself in a wilderness area and survive for prolonged periods if you have to.

Fire and Water

The aftermath of an emergency is likely to be as hazardous as the emergency itself. You may be able to react very well to a crisis situation, saving yourself from it, only to find a whole new set of problems of a long-term nature.

For example, you might be on an afternoon canoe trip in a part of the country that you are not familiar with. Suppose the canoe is ripped open by a jagged rock. You keep your head, manage to swim to shore, and even manage to hold on to some essentials such as matches and warm clothing. But suddenly you realize you are stranded: The canoe cannot be repaired, you are on your own many miles from your starting point, unsure of which direction to walk in to find help, and soaking wet and shivering. How do you cope? The immediate threat to your life is over, but other problems of survival are just beginning. We will look at these problems, in order of priority, in this and the next three chapters.

NO MATCHES?

On all but the very warmest summer nights, a fire is the difference between comfort and misery if you have no tent or sleeping bag. In cases of exposure or shock, it is essential to be able to build a fire to keep warm. If your clothes are soaked with water, it is very important, even in temperate weather, to be able to dry them out properly before continuing. Last but by no means least, a fire provides a boost to morale. Fire is a living, cheerful thing, a companion to drive away the darkness and keep up one's spirits. Outdoors, it is by no means an unnecessary luxury.

Bearing this in mind, you should naturally always carry matches in a waterproof, unbreakable container. You should, in fact, carry *two* supplies, in separate containers, in case one becomes lost.

If you are stuck without matches, you may wonder if it's possible to create fire by the rubbing-two-sticks-together method. The answer is "no"—unless you have already practiced the art a great deal and also are carrying some powdery-dry wood shavings, essential ingredients to bring the first spark to life.

There *are,* however, a few practical ways to create fire without matches. If you are ever stranded with an automobile, you can use the electrical energy that is stored in the automobile battery. Disconnect the wires from the battery, if possible; ideally, take the battery out from under the hood altogether. Attach a length of fence wire, or wire ripped out of the car (for example, the semi-exposed wires leading through the trunk lid to the rear lights), to each battery terminal. If you touch the wires together—carefully!—a lot of heat and sparks will be produced, easily enough to ignite paper, dry leaves, or small dead twigs.

A camera lens can be used to start a fire in bright sunlight. The wider the lens opening, the more heat it will produce. Open the back of the camera and hold the camera shutter open (if there is no setting for this, you will have to use a stick to jam the shutter open, inside the camera). Hold the open camera back up to the sun and focus the sunlight to a bright white point, about three inches below the camera lens. Use paper or dry leaves to start the fire and have dry twigs and wood ready to be added as soon as there are flames.

Spectacle lenses can be used the same way, though only glasses worn by a farsighted person will work. Nearsighted people wear glasses that are concave and will not focus light to a point.

BUILDING THE FIRE

If possible, find some large stones to make a bed for the fire and also to surround it, to protect it from strong wind and also to reflect the fire's heat toward you.

It is almost impossible to build a fire without something dry to burn to start with. If you are caught in the rain, search around close to the bases of trees or under leaves for small twigs that have not become wet. Make a little pyramid, around which you must build another pyramid of slightly larger twigs and fragments, around which you can stack full-size sticks. Camping supply stores sell combustible tablets—Hexamine, Heatabs—which are a lot of help.

Use enough wood to make a fair-sized pile; a bunch of twigs burns better than just a couple, since they radiate heat to each other. But stack the wood loosely, so that air can easily circulate through.

Gather more wood than you think you will need—fires have an amazing appetite. Always use dead wood, rather than rip live wood off trees; it burns better and is not destructive to nature.

PUTTING IT OUT

The trouble it takes to start the fire may make you laugh at the idea of having to take trouble to put it out. But once a fire has been burning for a while, it dries out and heats up the ground below and around it and can burn very persistently. You have a responsibility to be *certain* the fire is out before you leave it, so throw dirt on the flames and stamp the dirt down thoroughly, until not even a wisp of smoke is left.

IS IT SAFE
TO DRINK?

Besides keeping you warm and keeping you company, fire has another very important use—to sterilize water. We are so aware of pollution these days that you may find it hard to imagine drinking water from an open stream or river under any circum-

STARTING A CAMPFIRE

stances. But in a survival situation you are likely to be faced with the need to quench a thirst that you never realized could be so important to you; and if you are in a wilderness area, the water of a stream or river can almost certainly be made fit to drink.

Pollution of water can come from two different sources: chemical and organic. By "organic" we mean viruses and bacteria, resulting from animal wastes, decaying plant matter, or decaying animal flesh (for example, the water may flow over a dead muskrat upstream, picking up harmful bacteria on the way). Chemical pollution, on the other hand, generally comes only from man-made sources: the outlets of waste water from factories and city sewer systems. If you are in a survival situation you are unlikely to be downstream from a factory or a large town, so you can rule out chemical pollution of the water. (The only exception is in hot, dry areas such as the American Southwest, where there are some waterholes naturally contaminated with dangerous chemicals such as arsenic. Such dangerous water is easy to recognize, however, because there will be no green plants near it or in it, and there are likely to be bones of animals that were killed by drinking the water.)

It is difficult to remove chemical pollution from water, but, fortunately for you, it is easy to make organically polluted water fit to drink. One method is to boil it—for five minutes, plus an extra minute for each thousand feet you are above sea level. This will kill off the bacteria or viruses that may be present. Another method is to use water purification tablets—one per quart of water. These can be bought from camping supply stores or some drugstores. They must be kept in a tightly capped bottle to prevent deterioration. A couple of drops of iodine work the same way as a purification tablet; you can use either.

Suppose you have nothing to boil the water in or no purification tablets or iodine with you? Well, the water may be quite fit to drink anyway. Fast-running, narrow hillside and mountain streams are to be trusted more than slow-moving rivers. Try to follow the water back to its source, to check it out. Drink a small amount, ideally before you go to sleep, and wait to see if there are any side effects. If the water is not pure, probably the worst that you will experience is a slightly upset stomach. Incidentally, do not be put off by water that tastes strongly of minerals or is brackish or is not completely crystal clear. All these features are quite natural and do not mean the water is unfit to drink.

WATER OUT OF THIN AIR

If you are not near a stream or river, try collecting water out of the air. Dew is water that condenses from the air at night when the temperature goes down. It is guaranteed fit to drink. To collect it you will need to get up at dawn and mop up the dew with a piece of cloth, like a sponge. A heavy dew on long grass may yield as much as a quart of water this way, but it is hard work collecting it. A better way is to spread a sheet of plastic (your space blanket, if you have one) over a gentle depression you have scooped in the ground. Lay some small, cool rocks in the center of the plastic. (Rocks dug from at least a foot below the surface will be cool even in warm weather.) Dew will condense on them, run down, and collect in the middle of the plastic sheet. About one pint of water can be collected in this way. Needless to say, the plastic sheet also collects rainwater.

WATER IN THE DESERT

In hot, dry climates there is little or no dew that you can collect in the mornings. But there is some water in the ground that you can tap if you have a container to collect it in (a cup or a can) and a large sheet of plastic. In this case the plastic must be

COLLECTING DEW WITH A PLASTIC SHEET

transparent, so a space blanket (which has a silvered surface) will not work.

A hole is scooped in the ground, about two feet deep and four feet wide. The water container is placed in the center of the hole, and the plastic sheet is then spread over the hole, its edges held down by rocks or sand. The center of the plastic should sag so that it is close to, but does not quite touch, the mouth of the container underneath. A rock placed in the middle of the sheet will keep it in the right position.

Sunlight shining through the plastic creates warmth in the gap under it, vaporizing water in the surrounding earth or sand. This vaporized water then rises and condenses on the underside of the plastic, running down and dripping off into the container.

The setup should yield up to three pints of water a day. Since the body requires about a gallon of water per day in desert regions, you will need three "water pumps" working to provide enough water for continued survival. The water does not need to be purified, since it is distilled in the process of being collected.

WATER AT SEA

If you are ever stranded at sea, it is more than likely you will remember seeing a movie or reading a book in which some survivors in a lifeboat give in to temptation and try to quench their thirsts with seawater—and die horribly as a result. You will wonder whether this is really fact or fiction. Surely, salt water cannot be so dangerous?

Unfortunately, this is a case of folklore turning out to be true. Although the body in fact needs some intake of salt to maintain good health, the large amounts of salt in seawater overload the system, and the body responds by actually drawing on its reserves of water in the body tissues to wash the excess salt away. This means that if you drink seawater, after a short-lived feeling of relief from thirst, you will suddenly be

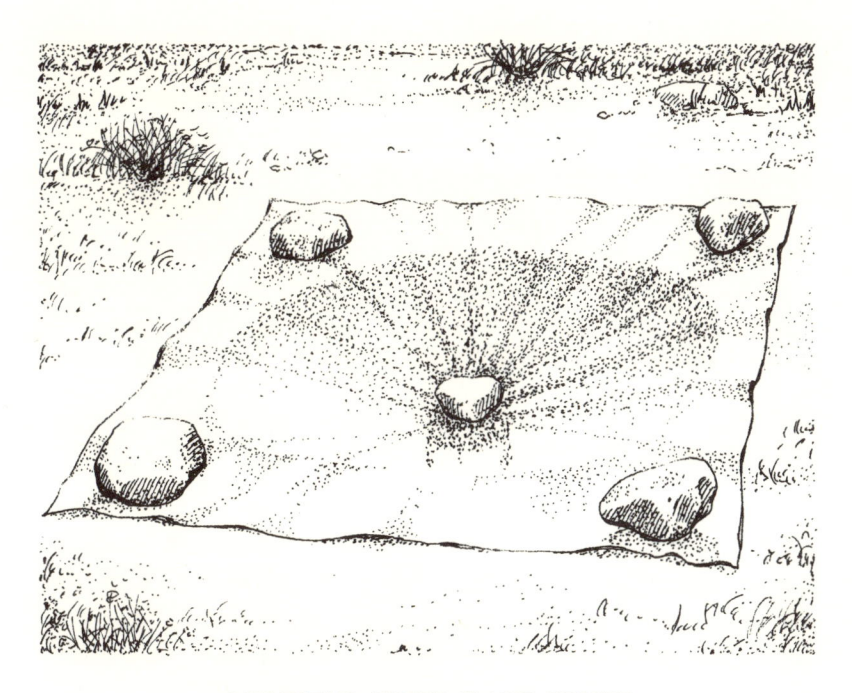

COLLECTING WATER IN THE DESERT

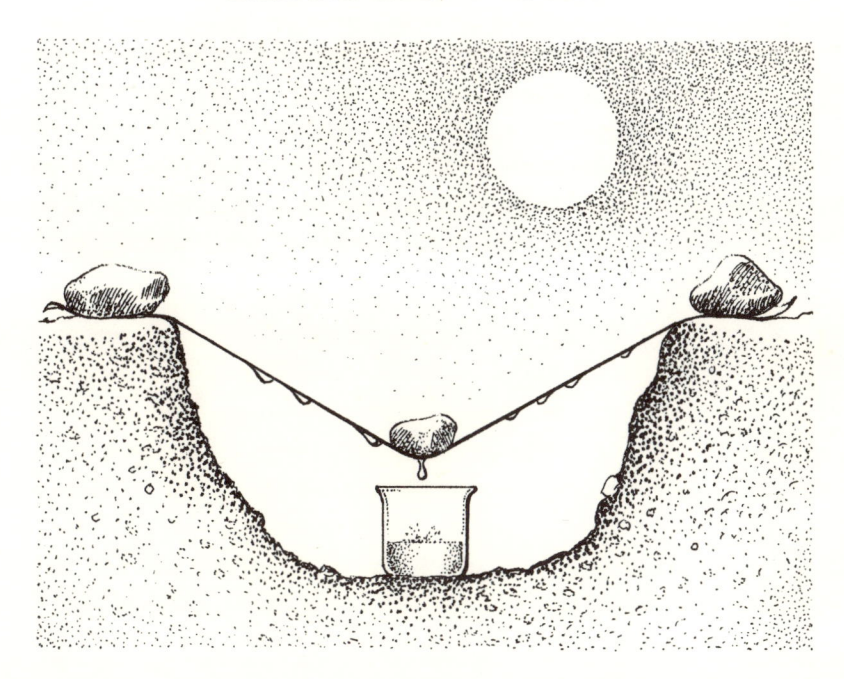

worse off than before, requiring still more water to get rid of the excess salt. Drinking more seawater loads more salt into the body again, and the process becomes a vicious circle. Death follows quickly, from dehydration.

The *only* kind of seawater that is safe to drink is sea ice that has been frozen for one year or more. The older it is, the less salty it becomes (test by tasting). Old sea ice is blue and has blunt corners when it breaks. New sea ice is gray-white and fragments into sharp shards.

WATER SUBSTITUTES

Thirsty people resort to desperate measures. Thirst becomes such an overwhelming sensation that it obscures common sense. As a result, there are cases of people who die from drinking water from their car radiator (usually containing antifreeze, which is a poison) or from their car battery (very acidic, and impossible to make safe to drink). In a desperate situation you may try drinking beer or wine, since both contain a high proportion of water, but the alcohol will tend to produce a false state of confidence and well-being, leading to mistakes being made—possibly fatally. And hard liquor should never be used to quench thirst since, like seawater, it actually tends to dehydrate the body and leaves you worse off than before. As in all survival situations, you must never let desperation cloud your judgment.

Finding Food

WHAT DO YOU NEED?

Studies with army volunteers have shown that if a person in good physical shape is kept supplied with water, he can manage to go for amazingly long periods of time without food. Hunger pangs subside after the first day or two. Weakness and dizziness gradually become more severe, but survival for up to a month without any food intake is not unusual.

It is one thing to read about this, however, and quite another thing to find yourself in a real-life situation, experiencing it. No one will starve to death deprived of food intake for a few days, but this doesn't mean it will be pleasant! More important from the point of view of survival, strength and stamina quickly diminish without food intake, and so does morale. So, even though finding food is not such an absolute necessity as keeping warm and finding water, it makes good sense to itemize some of the easiest food sources available to someone who is stranded in a wilderness area.

IS IT POISONOUS?

There are edible plants all around, in fields and forests, but there is no absolutely surefire way of telling them apart from those that are *not* safe to eat. A common mistake is to think that anything an animal eats will be safe for a human being; in reality horses enjoy munching poison ivy, squirrels are unharmed by poisonous mushrooms, and birds eat poisonous berries.

Rather than trying to memorize the plants that are poisonous, your safest bet is to memorize a few common varieties that are safe. Some of these are listed below. In addition, there are some basic rules about plants you should definitely avoid:

1. Don't eat *any* kind of mushroom. Not only is it hard even for experts to identify which mushrooms are poisonous, but mushrooms have almost zero food value anyway. They may taste good, but they are not nutritious.

2. Don't eat any plant that irritates the skin, has an irritating smell, or has milky juice inside it.

3. Do not eat any plants found growing near railroad tracks—even if you know the plants are normally edible. Vegetation near railroad tracks is often sprayed with weed killers that are poisonous.

SOME SAFE BETS

Dandelions and clover may seem better suited as food for cows than for people, but in fact these common plants have saved many lives in times of famine. The whole of each plant is edible, including flowers and roots. Young clover can be eaten raw—its taste is not unpleasant—but dandelions are best boiled, if possible, to reduce their bitterness. Their roots should be peeled before cooking, although this is not essential.

Cattails (scientific name, *Typhaceae*) are another common weed that is easily recognized and good to eat. They are also known as bulrushes or cat-o'-nine-tails. Their "flower" (a tubular husk that gradually turns brown through the summer) can be eaten as you would corn. Their stems can be peeled and eaten like asparagus, and their roots (again, after peeling) are particularly good, being high in starch content. All the parts of the plant are edible raw, though more palatable if cooked for a while.

Members of the knotweed famiy (there are about thirty different species, similar to one another in appearance) are likewise good to eat, and you can compile a long list of other safe plants by studying a lay guide to botany. From the survival point of view, however, you are better off looking for nuts and berries rather than green plants, since they usually supply more calories. All nuts are edible, so you need have no hesi-

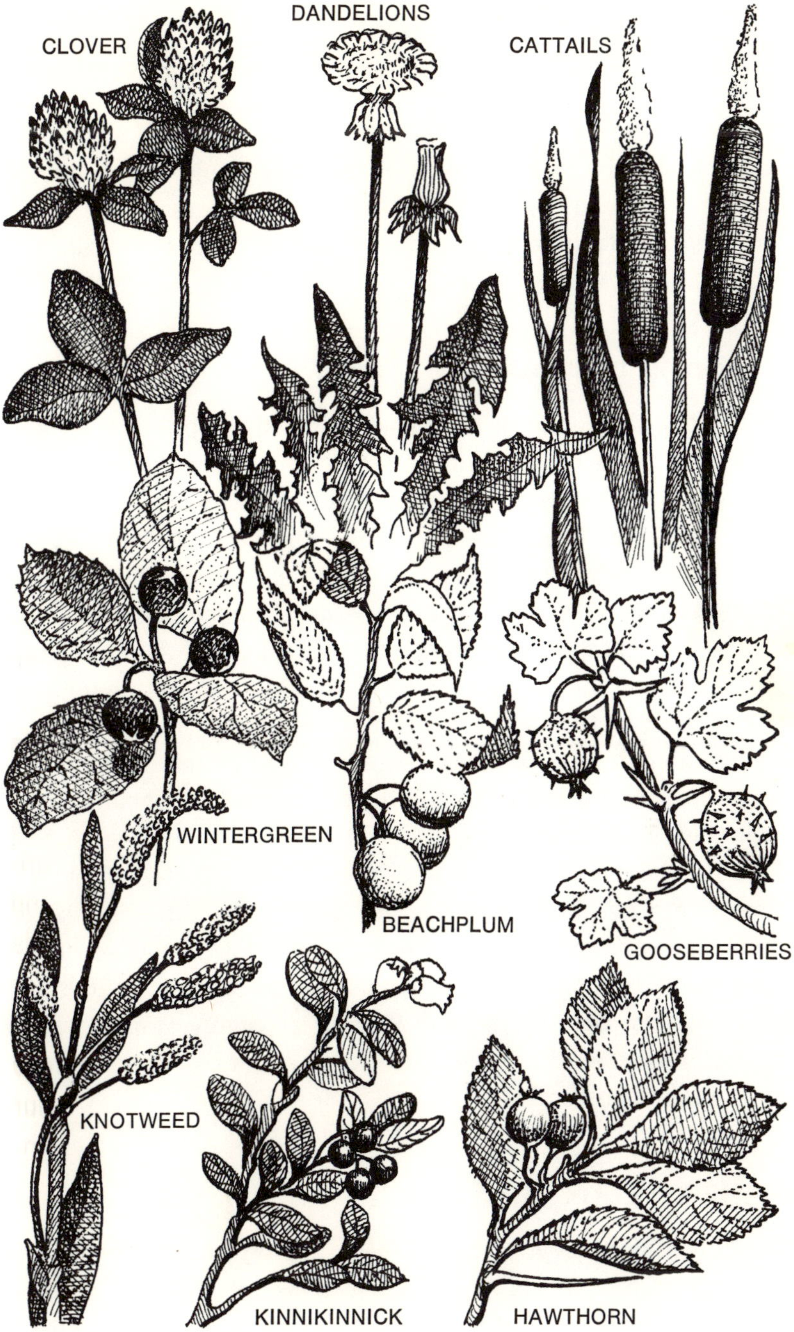

DANDELIONS
CLOVER
CATTAILS
WINTERGREEN
BEACHPLUM
GOOSEBERRIES
KNOTWEED
KINNIKINNICK
HAWTHORN

tation, even if they tend to taste bitter. (This bitterness can be lessened if you are able to chop the nuts up and wash the fragments in running water.) Some berries are poisonous, but you can feel safe eating those from wintergreen and kinnikinnick and the fruit of hawthorn and beach plum. You should not be surprised if you stumble on even more familiar species growing wild: blueberries, strawberries, gooseberries, and grapes.

IF YOU'RE DESPERATE...

If you can find none of the basic plants described above, and hunger is gnawing away, there are some emergency foods that are less pleasant to eat but should not be ruled out.

The inner layers of tree bark, for instance, are usually edible; avoid it only if it tastes extremely bitter. Ferns (especially young ones) are generally safe. Lichens can be eaten if you can scrape them from the rocks on which they grow. And seaweed that is young and fresh is safe to eat, though its saltiness (it tastes like fresh raw fish) will make you thirsty.

In an emergency, faced with some berries that *look* edible, even though you can't identify them, you can try some experimentally. Take one berry, break it open with your teeth and hold it between your lips and teeth for a few minutes. If, by this time, there has been no soapy or burning or extremely bitter taste developing in your mouth, eat just a few of the berries—then wait. Ten hours is a good, safe period of time. If you have no ill-effects (bearing in mind that on an empty stomach sour berries of any kind are liable to cause slight discomfort), consider the berries edible.

WHERE TO LOOK

You can maximize your chances of finding edible plants by knowing where the plants are most likely to be found. Water is the first essential, so follow sloping land down into dips, hollows, and valleys, where the pickings will be richer. Plants (with some exceptions) grow less successfully when competing side-by-side with trees, so you should try to avoid heavily forested areas of land. On the other hand, if you find an area that was recently cleared of trees, the pickings will be particularly good, as vegetation springs up in the soil where trees used to grow. Blueberries are common here. Around the edges of a wood or forest look for gooseberries, though they may be difficult to get at among dense vegetation.

EATING ANIMALS

There are many species of poisonous or indigestible plants, or plants that have no food value, but almost every part of every animal in America is edible, nutritious, and relatively high in calories. We do not expect that overnight you can become a hunter or even a trapper; catching game and knowing how to prepare and cook it once it has been caught are skills that take time to learn and develop and require a fair amount of experience in the wilds.

However, there are some easy ways of catching some species, and hunger will make any survivor less fussy about how nicely his food is prepared.

First, remember that insects are edible, and in fact are considered delicacies in some parts of the world. Grasshoppers are tasty when roasted after removing wings and legs. Ants, also, are said to be good, especially large black ants that live in rotten or hollow logs. Larvae, earthworms, termites— you may imagine that you are too squeamish ever to chew and swallow this kind of "food," but squeamishness decreases as desperation increases, and insects are certainly easy to find and catch.

Next easiest, probably, are fish. If you have your survival kit with you, and it contains some fishhooks and a length of line, fine; if you don't, you should probably forget about trying to catch trout, catfish, or pike by "tickling" them—sneaking up and touching the belly of the fish until it is hypnotized and can be lifted out of the water. It's even harder than it sounds, and your time will be better spent looking for other forms of food. Likewise, fishing with a length of vine and a bent pin is liable to be unrewarding. Even if a fish is caught in this way, it will tend to fall off the pin before you manage to land it.

If you do have fishing equipment and manage to make a catch, kill the landed fish by clubbing it or slitting it from gill to gill. Remove the fish scales by scraping with the top, dull edge of a knife blade. Note that a catfish's back fins are poisonous, delivering an unpleasant sting.

Unhealthy fish should not be eaten. Beware of specimens with flabby skin, slimy gills, or sunken eyes. Beware of live fish that smell unpleasant. Another test: Press your thumb into the fish; if the dent produced stays there, don't eat the fish.

Similarly, some shellfish should be left alone. A live shellfish clinging to a rock should move when you touch it, trying to cling still tighter. Shellfish that don't have this reaction should be left alone. Also shellfish with cone-shaped shells are likely to be inedible.

Moving from water onto land, an animal that is easy to catch and little trouble to prepare is the frog. They can most easily be tracked down at night, when they are noisiest. A light will catch a frog's attention; it should be possible to grab it barehanded. Before eating it you will have to skin it, but the whole of its insides are edible—and, some say, delicious.

Other wildlife is less likely to stand still to be caught. Your chances are increased at night; sleeping birds, for instance, can be taken from their nests, perhaps with a loop of wire on the end of a stick. Many animals are attracted, and mesmerized, by a flashlight.

None of this is good hunting practice, or even legal hunting practice, and should be resorted to only when you are desperate for food. Even then, you will need to be hardhearted to be able to kill and skin what you catch.

COOK IT FIRST

Even the plants that are edible raw will taste better, and be easier to digest, if they are cooked for a while. "Easier to digest" means that your body may extract more food value, so cooking is practical as well as pleasant. Also, some—but not all—poisonous plants are made harmless by being boiled.

If you have no water container, there are three alternative cooking methods at your disposal. You can bury your food in earth or clay directly under the fire; baked in this way, plants and vegetables will cook in about twenty minutes, fish and meat take longer. Wrap small morsels in leaves to keep them clean and manageable. The cooking time is measured from when the fire becomes hot and vigorous, incidentally—usually about fifteen minutes after lighting it.

Alternatively, you can roast your food over the flames—not so easy, since it will tend to burn on the surface and remain raw inside. Or, you can smother the food with the fire's hot glowing embers. This, too, is less easy to control—the heat may be too great, leaving you with an unappetizing meal of black powder. Baking, though most time-consuming, is easiest.

Finding Your Way

Even a mountain guide will walk in wide, endless circles if blindfolded and wandering in an area that he is not familiar with. It is true that some people have a better sense of direction than others, but there is nothing mysterious about this "sense." It is simply a matter of taking notice, consciously or unconsciously, of your surroundings. A guide has a heightened awareness of every tiny visual cue telling him which way he is facing, and whether he has seen a place before. You may not have the talent to develop such total awareness yourself, but you can certainly improve your ability by concentrating and keeping track of your surroundings.

SET OUT OR STAY PUT?

The first question, however, is whether you should try to find your way to help or home at all. You must take stock of your situation and evaluate your chances. Do you know how far you will have to travel? Do you know what the terrain is like? Are you used to walking that kind of distance? Is the weather good or bad? If you stay put, do you have any food or water? Did you tell anyone where you were going—in which case, how long will it take them to come out looking for you and will they know where to look? If no one knows where you are, how likely is it that someone may pass close by accidentally, within reach of a shout for help or the sight of a fire or flashlight? Is your position sheltered and warm? If so, it may be wiser to stay where you are than risk a long trek through rain or snow. If you stay put you face eventual starvation; if you set out, you will exhaust your reserves of energy much faster, especially if you are already injured.

Finally, after taking all these factors into consideration,

you will have to estimate the most important factor of all: your own strength and abilities. Only then can you make a sensible decision.

KEEPING TRACK

When you decide to try to walk to safety, from wherever you have found yourself stranded, it is essential that you make a careful, logical decision about which direction to set out in, and then *keep* to that direction. There are several rule-of-thumb methods to keep track of your progress and direction of movement.

If you have paper and pencil with you, make a map as you go along, pausing now and then to put in significant landmarks. This will enable you to retrace your steps accurately if you have to (for instance, if you come up against a steep slope that can't be climbed and must be gone around). It will also stop you from feeling lost.

Try to be aware of the contours of the land. It is often a safe bet to follow a river, since water moves consistently downhill (which will mean easier walking for you), and when the country was first colonized, people tended to build houses and villages near water sources; so, if you are totally lost, your odds of eventually finding help will be improved by sticking close to any fair-sized river. On the other hand, water seldom takes the *shortest* path, and by staying down in the valleys you will lose the opportunity to gain perspective from high vantage points. You will have to weigh the relative merits involved.

If you are striking straight across country and want to maintain your direction accurately, the procedure is to choose two points that both lie ahead on your line of travel. Walk so that the two points remain lined up with one another, from your point of view. Then, before you reach the first point, choose another—a particular tree, a rock formation—that is in line with and beyond the first two. Keep repeating this procedure and you should not deviate too much from your chosen path.

When you sit down to rest, it is a good idea to indicate to yourself the direction in which you have been traveling. An arrow scratched in the earth, or a straight piece of wood laid beside you, will do. Otherwise, you may rest for ten minutes and then get up only to find you can't remember exactly which way you have been heading.

Finding your way becomes more of a problem in forests. The surrounding trees can begin to seem almost alive with hostility and menace. Should you follow a path if you find one? This is not always an easy decision. Forests are full of misleading path-like segments that sooner or later disappear into impenetrable undergrowth. If you find a well-worn track made by forest animals, you should try following it if it seems to have been used recently. A better way of keeping a sense of direction under the trees is by leaving marks behind you—notches cut into tree trunks or, if you have no knife, vines or long grasses wound round or hung from tree limbs. Walk so that you keep your marked trees lined up behind you, the same way you would keep landmarks lined up ahead of you.

The more you walk outdoors, the more confidence you will have. Look at everything, and listen, and feel. It is possible to hear the differences in the sound of the wind, to smell the differences between moist and dry ground, to sense your altitude, and to feel the differences in the texture of the ground you walk on. Living in urban or suburban areas our senses of these subtle qualities are not needed, so we forget how to use them. After walking outdoors for a while, consciously making yourself aware of everything around you, you will be surprised how much your senses can tell you.

DIRECTIONAL AIDS

So far, we have dealt only with ways of keeping your direction that depend on using the landscape around you. At times when there are thick, heavy clouds, the landscape will be your only guide, so you should indeed know how to use it for information. But when the sky is clear, the sun and stars are also there to help you.

Many people are under the impression that after rising in the East, the sun travels through the sky directly overhead, passing through a point vertically above at noon, before heading for the West. In fact, at all times of the year in northern latitudes (which includes the whole United States), the sun takes a curving path through the sky toward the South, on its way to the West. At noon the sun will be almost due south, depending on how you are positioned in your time zone. And, of course, you must allow for "summer time," when clocks are artificially set one hour ahead so that we can enjoy longer evenings. If your watch is running on summer time, the sun will shine from the south around 1 P.M., not noon.

IMPROVISED SUNDIAL

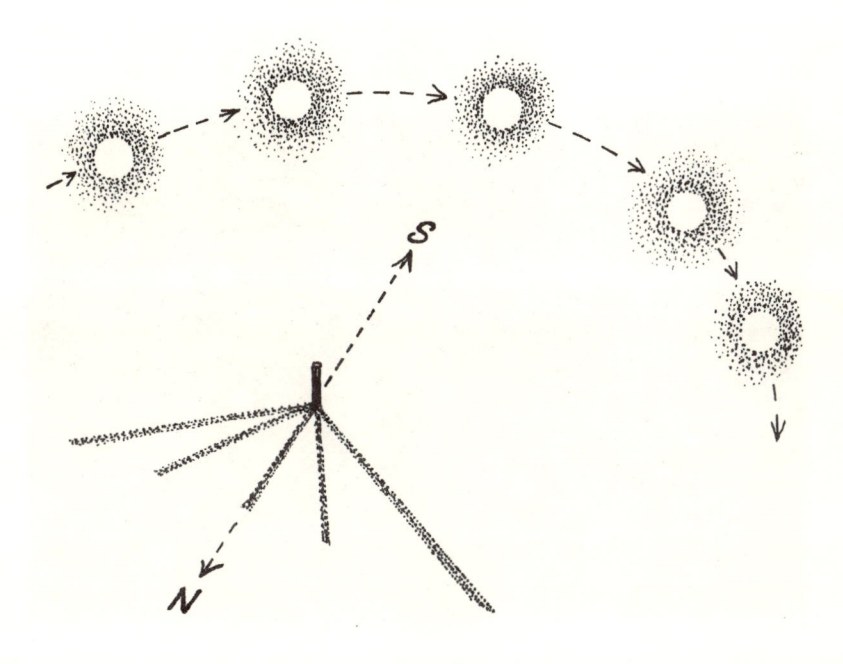

It may be hard to figure out which way the sun is moving when it is quite high in the sky. The easiest method is to hold a stick at right angles to the ground and observe the direction of the shadow. The shadow will be shortest when the sun is due south, so if you have the time to sit and make periodic examinations of the length of the shadow, you can locate due south even if you have no watch.

At night, you should know how to locate the polestar, Polaris. This is the star at the end of the "handle" of the Little Dipper constellation. Another way to locate it is to find the Big Dipper and imagine a line drawn out, upward, from the two stars at the end of the "dipper" part. This imaginary line leads to the polestar.

All the other stars in the sky, and the planets, move as time passes, but the polestar remains so nearly motionless that for all practical purposes it can be used for an accurate guide, when you want to know which way is true north (as opposed to magnetic north—see next section).

LOCATING THE POLESTAR

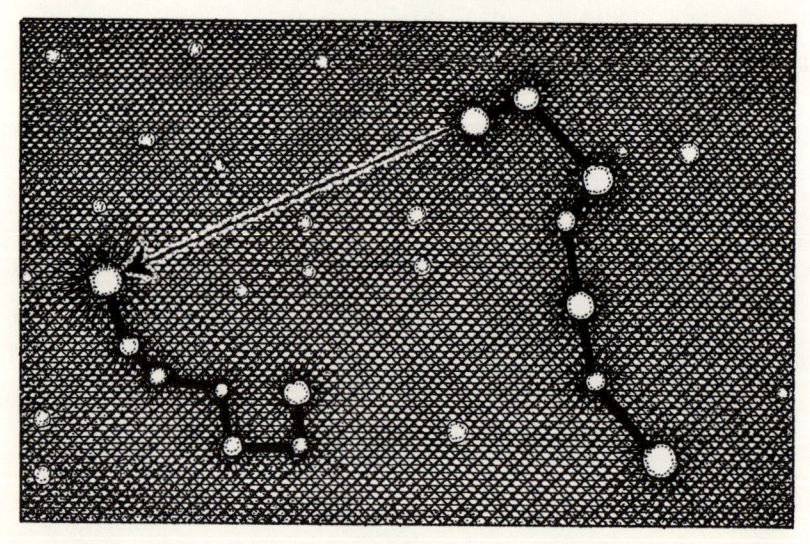

THE COMPASS

If you have a compass with you, your problems are over—provided, of course, you know how to *use* the compass! Here is a short guide describing the basic method.

Compasses consist either of a swinging needle, which is magnetized so that it tends to point to the earth's magnetic north, or a turning magnetized disk, like the needle but with full markings on it showing north, south, east, and west. Better compasses have either the disk or needle enclosed in a liquid-filled chamber; the liquid damps down the compass's tendency to swing to and fro before coming to rest.

When using a compass, first pick out a landmark in the direction that you want to travel. It should be as far off as possible. Then hold the compass so that its needle, or the north mark on its disk, lines up exactly with the magnetic north marked on the compass's case, in which the disk or needle is free to turn. Next sight across the compass (with its disk or needle still lined up with the north mark on its case) to see where the line of sight of your landmark crosses the calibration marked in degrees around the edges of the compass's case. (Toy compasses whose cases are not calibrated in degrees are almost impossible to use; don't bother buying one.) What you are doing is measuring the angle between your intended direction of travel and magnetic north. Magnetic north should remain constant, so if your direction of travel compared to it also remains constant, you will be heading in a straight line.

To make it easy to sight your landmark and read its direction while holding the compass, there are two kinds of instrument: the lensatic compass and the hinged mirror compass. The lensatic compass consists of a hinged disk that stands up vertically and a lens opposite the disk. Look through the lens, through a slit in the disk, at your landmark. The lens enables you to read the compass dial at the same time you have your landmark in view. Check that the compass is still

TWO COMPASS TYPES

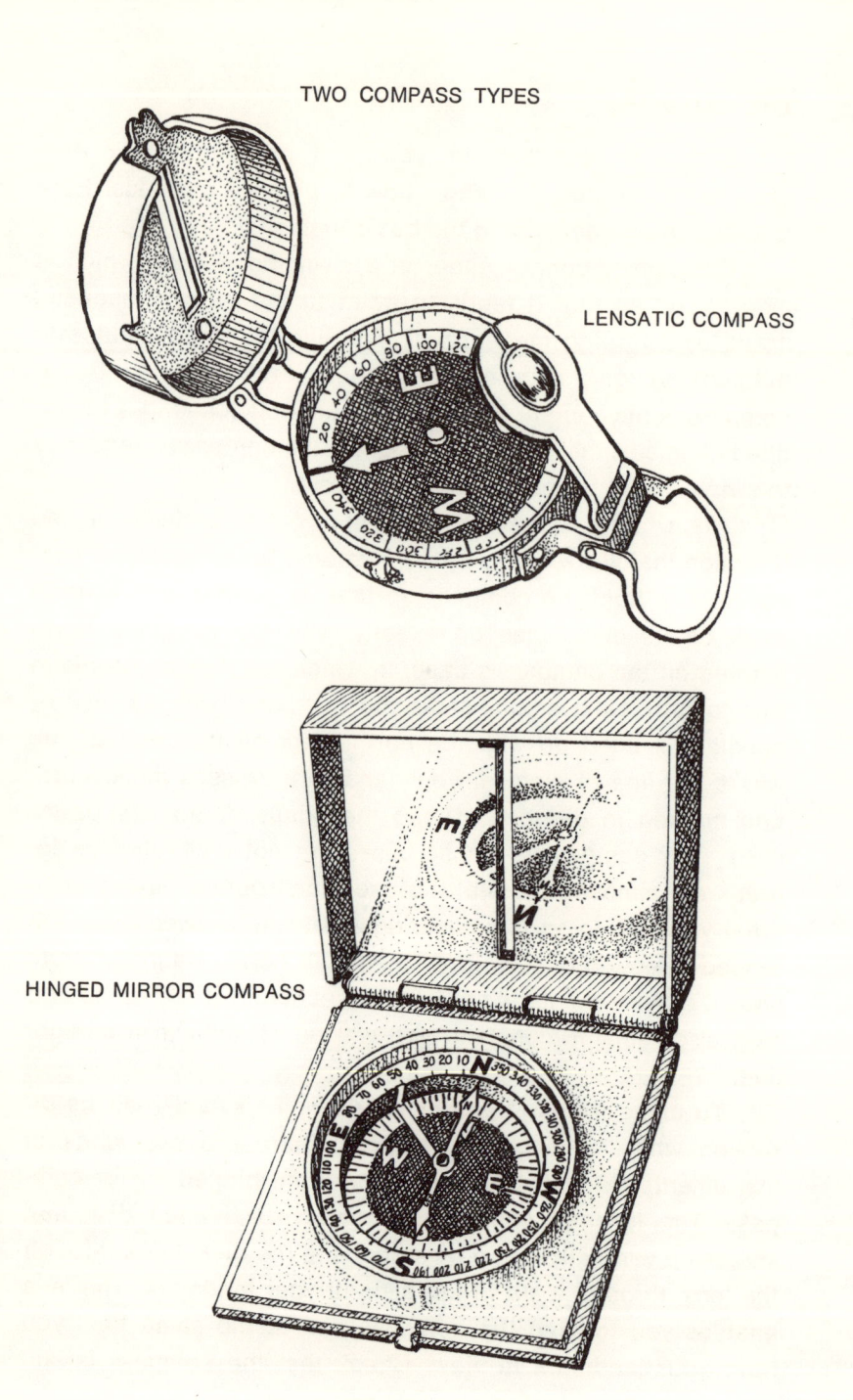

LENSATIC COMPASS

HINGED MIRROR COMPASS

pointing to the north mark on its case, then take your reading. At any time, from then on, you can stop, take out the compass, set it to north, and check to see that you are still walking in the same direction compared to north.

The hinged mirror compass employs a mirror to reflect an image of the compass dial so that you can see the dial at the same time that you are sighting your landmark in the mirror (similar to procedure with the lensatic compass). The hinged mirror compass is easy to use for people who wear glasses, since it has no lens that must be peered through.

POINTS TO REMEMBER

We have talked a lot about how to avoid getting lost if you try to walk back to safety after an accident or emergency. But your determination to keep heading in a straight line should be moderated with common sense. You will need all the energy you have, so it would be futile and foolish to force through a tangle of undergrowth, scale a cliff, or plow through a marshy area just to keep single-mindedly heading in the same direction. Detour around hazards and obstacles; even backtrack if necessary. Take the line of least resistance to conserve energy and get back on your true path after the obstacle is behind you. Whether you have a compass or are using the method of lining up two landscape features at a time in front of you, you can always rediscover your original direction.

Generally, when walking to safety, you should be more cautious than at any other time, since you will be in no position to be able to afford having an accident. When descending steep slopes, tend to lean slightly backward, so that if you slip you will fall back rather than ahead, down the slope. Try to avoid routes that involve a lot of ascending and descending of land; this takes a great deal more energy. Resist the temptation to go all-out; instead, maintain a steady, methodical pace and rest for a couple of minutes now and then. These points may all seem obvious, until you are in a predicament and are anxious to reach security as soon as possible. Then, you may have to force yourself to remember the importance of common sense and taking it easy.

Staying Put and Signaling

Suppose that you and your friends or family are driving through a lonely part of the country when there is a severe snowstorm, forcing you to stop and immobilizing the car. You know your approximate position from a road map, but it is twenty miles to the nearest township marked on the map and for all you know there is no human habitation between you and it. To make things worse, none of you has particularly warm clothing. Inside the car you are safe and comfortable; you can run the motor for ten minutes every hour to keep the heater operating, and you can collect water by melting snow with the heat from the engine. But you are stranded, without food, and you doubt that anyone will happen along to find you, since the road now is so deep in snow that it is impassable for anything less than a Jeep with snow chains and a four-wheel drive.

The temptation to set out on foot, looking for help, is very strong under these circumstances. There are many cases of people who do just that, regardless of their lack of proper clothing and the exhausting nature of a walk through deep snow. In most of these cases, the adventurers freeze to death as a result of their foolishness.

An automobile is an ideal shelter and should not be abandoned hastily, especially if friends or family are expecting you. When you don't turn up, they will realize you must have run into difficulties and will sound the alarm. There are many other similar situations when you should stay put instead of setting out to find help—if you have broken a leg or ankle in an accident, for example.

But how will anyone find you? Assuming you have good reason to believe that people will start looking for you or that the region is sufficiently well-traveled for someone to be likely to pass by eventually, there are a number of steps you can take to make your position visible.

FIRES

If you can move around at all, the first step you should take is to gather wood for three fires. Three, because this is recognized as a distress signal. In daytime, try to make the fires smoke as much as possible by piling on green wood or wet leaves, moss, car tires, or the oil from a car engine. (However, if you are relying on the engine to work the automobile heater to keep you warm, this is more important.) At night, try to make the fires as bright as possible. Keep extra fuel handy to throw on the fires if you hear a low-flying airplane (the large, high-flying jets won't see you anyway, so ignore them).

If you find a dead tree, sufficiently isolated from other trees, lighting the tree itself can make a beacon. Birchbark, too, is excellent for producing quick, bright flames.

SYMBOLS AND SIGNALS

In snow, it is easy to form giant letters that will be visible from high up. Plow the furrows as deep and as wide as possible, forming an S-O-S or an arrow pointing to your stranded position. Make your letters or symbols up to forty feet long and ten feet thick. An "X" means "unable to proceed," and an "F" distress marking means you need food and water. Two parallel lines— | | , like a vertical "equals" sign—mean you need medical supplies.

Furrows that have been dug into the earth are equally visible when the sun is shining. Signal your presence in as many ways as possible: a bright cloth tied to the car's radio antenna, a pile of tree branches, anything that will show up as something out of keeping with the natural environment.

If you have a whistle, three blasts on it is a distress signal. Likewise, three gunshots if you have a gun.

Some survival kits contain brightly colored fabric or plastic strips that can be laid out on the ground in the form of a symbol or used like flags, hung from a high point. Some kits may contain a bright-colored, highly concentrated powdered dye, which can be spread thinly on the ground or dropped into a lake or slow-running river.

MIRROR SIGNALING

Reflected sunlight from a mirror can be visible to even a high-flying airplane, and if you can flash an S-O-S (three shorts, three longs, three shorts) you can make it clear that the flashes are not just accidental.

You may be able to find an army signaling mirror in a surplus store, which will be cheaper than buying a new one (available in larger camping equipment stores). Either way, for you to be able to send proper signals, it really has to be designed for the job. A signaling mirror is double-sided and has a small clear spot in the middle. To use it, look through the clear spot at your target while holding the mirror at arm's length. Then, if your target is relatively close to the sun's position, move the mirror until you see (in the mirrored side that is toward you) the spot of sunlight that comes through the clear part of the mirror and falls on your face. Turn the mirror until this sunlight spot moves to appear to coincide with the center of the mirror and disappears in the clear area there. If you are still sighting your target through the clear area, in this position the outer mirrored side of the signaling mirror will reflect sunlight directly at the target.

If the sun is more than 90 degrees from your target, hold the signaling mirror so that the sun shines through the clear spot and falls on the palm of your hand. Then line up this point of sunlight, as seen in the mirror, in exactly the same way

USING A SIGNALING MIRROR

that you lined up the spot of sunlight that fell on your face. This description sounds complicated, but in practice it is easy to follow.

If you don't have a signaling mirror, but do have an ordinary mirror, move it around randomly, hoping to flash sunlight in the direction of any airplane you see or hear. The end of a tin can or a sheet of aluminum foil will do almost as well.

MAINTAINING MORALE

We have talked a lot at different points about maintaining morale, but it is probably harder to keep your spirits up when you are stranded or staying put than it is at any other time. Sitting around and waiting for rescue is bound to be demoralizing. You are doing nothing concrete to save yourself. Time is passing, hunger is becoming intolerable, and it is easy to begin imagining a dozen different horrible deaths.

The best answer is to keep yourself occupied, as much as your physical condition will allow. Set yourself small tasks—building bigger signal fires, gathering more supplies of food and water, improving your shelter—and carry them out slowly and thoroughly, concentrating on the job at hand. If you want to avoid physical exertion to conserve energy, set yourself mental tasks—mental arithmetic, lists of the names of everyone you have ever known in your life, and so on. Be alert for signs of someone coming to rescue you but try not to become obsessed with this. Doing nothing may seem a foolish and useless way to improve your chances of survival, but you must remind yourself of people whose willpower and common sense were not strong enough to keep them from setting out in a desperate and ill-considered attempt to reach help—with the result that they never made it.

Once you have made your decision to stay put, stick to it. That decision was probably made when you were at your most rational and least panicky; let it guide you, a day or two days or even a week later, when increasing desperation threatens to cloud good judgment.

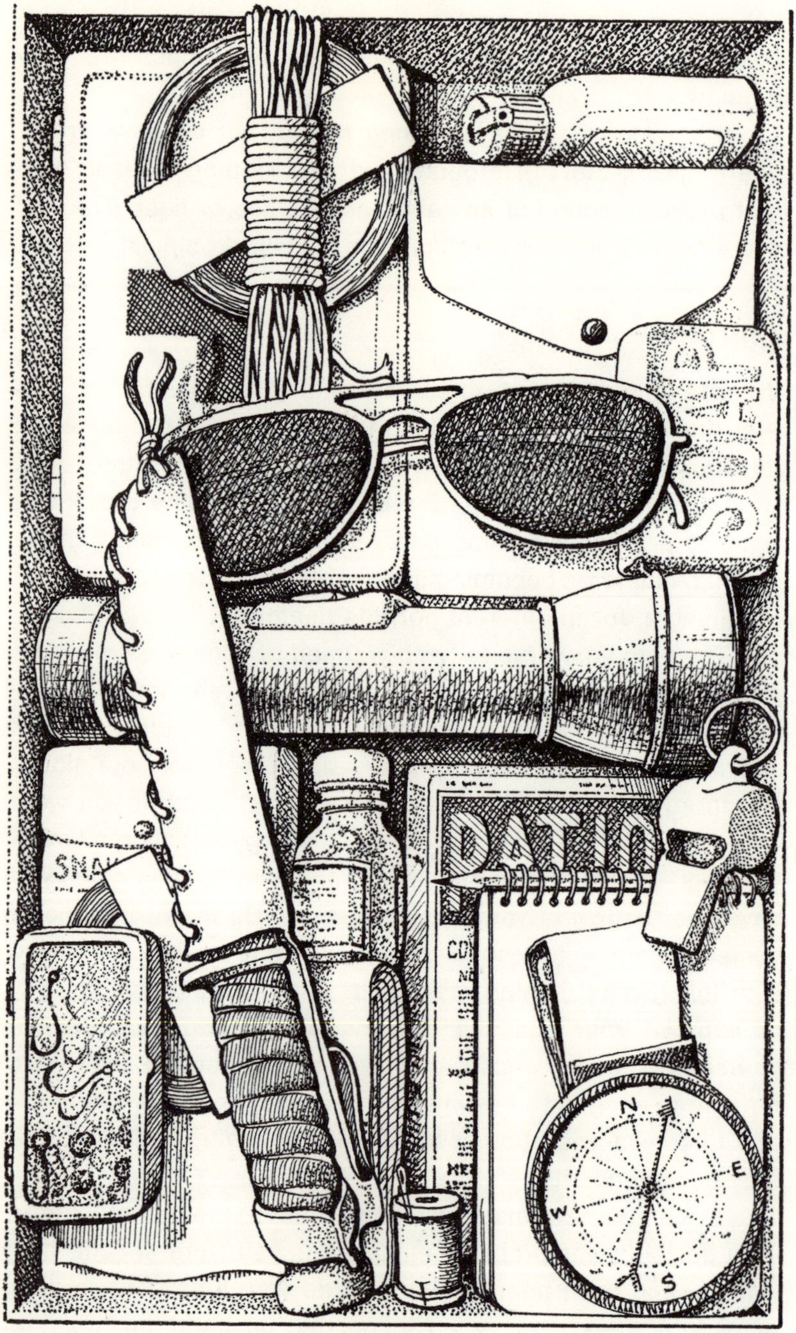
SOAP
N
E
S
W

Appendix 1: Your Survival Kit

You can buy commercially made survival kits in camping stores. None of them will contain *all* the items in the following list, but they are a convenient way of providing yourself with some of the essentials, and they are compact and lightweight. To carry items you have gathered together yourself, use a flexible plastic box that is wide, flat, and watertight. Alternatively, a really heavy-duty plastic bag can be used.

Matches
Keep one set of wooden kitchen matches in your kit and another set in a plastic box of their own, separately. They are essential.

Compass
It should be waterproof and durable enough to withstand the wear-and-tear of being carried in your pocket and dropped occasionally, and it should have a luminous pointer and numerals.

Glasses
If you need prescription lenses to see where you are going, consider carrying a spare pair of glasses with you.

Plastic
The space blanket, mentioned earlier, is obtainable from camping stores and keeps you warm in an emergency. It will also collect water. Since you can't use it for both operations at once, also have on hand a six-foot square of thin Mylar plastic (sold in camping stores or as covers to protect clothes from dust, motorcycles from rain, etc.); it should be thin enough to fold into a parcel that will fit into a shirt pocket.

Knife
A sheath knife with a leather case is more versatile than a clasp knife.

Snakebite Kit
Instructions for its use are included in it.

Fishing Gear
Several yards of line, half a dozen small hooks, a few lead sinkers—and nothing else.

Insect Repellent

Paper and Pencil

Flashlight
A light powered by two D cells is ideal.

Whistle
A referee whistle—to sound a distress signal.

Water Purification Tablets
They deteriorate with age, so replace them if they are more than a year old. Obtainable from drugstores. Iodine may be used instead, so don't bother with tablets if iodine is in your medical kit (see below).

Cord and Wire
A small coil of piano wire and a good length of nylon cord (like parachute cord) come in handy in many different situations.

Soap
To wash any cut or scrape to prevent infection.

Rations
Check out the emergency rations that are available from camping supply stores. If you take food of your own with you, remember that fats contain more available calories than almost any other form of food and should definitely be included along with carbohydrates.

Needle and Thread

Not an absolute essential, but convenient, if clothing is severely ripped. Torn clothing is ineffective as insulation from the weather.

Medical Kit

Aspirin and Band-Aids are obvious essentials. To disinfect wounds you may consider using iodine, but an antibiotic cream such as Auromycin is more effective and comes in small, convenient tubes. Include two rolls of gauze bandages—one small and narrow, the other long and wide. A small tube of ointment for insect stings or burns. And ask your physician for the following prescription drugs, for use in any possible emergency when you are isolated from help: Ampicillin capsules, to fight any major infection, resulting, for instance, from a wound; Lomotil tablets, to reduce the effects of gastroenteritis or other stomach upset producing diarrhea, which can be severely debilitating unless controlled. This is especially true if you don't have enough water to replace the fluids that are lost.

Appendix 2: Sources of Supply

First, buy a few camping and outdoors magazines and look at the advertisements to give yourself an idea of the range of equipment being offered and the prices.

Then visit your local camping store or, if one is not within easy reach, write for catalogs from the following outfitters, which carry large selections:

Co-op Wilderness Shop, Oakland Cooperative, 3601 Allies Boulevard, Pittsburgh, PA 15213

Eastern Mountain Sports, Inc., 1041 Commonwealth Avenue, Boston, MA 02215

Highland Outfitters, P.O. Box 121, Riverside, CA 92502

Index

Altostratus clouds, 9
Aluminum foil, for signaling, 53
Animals, wild, danger from, 14
    as food, 37–38
Ants, 37
Avalanches, 14–15

Backstroke, 17
Band-Aids, for blisters, 15
Bears, 14
Bee sting, 16
Berries, 34–36
Big Dipper, 44
Blisters, 4, 15
Blueberries, 36, 37
Body temperature, 11–12
Breaststroke, 17, 18
Bug repellant cream, 16

Camera lens, for making fires, 24
Canada, 5, 6
Carbohydrates, 14
Catfish, 37
Cattails, 34
Chambers of commerce, free literature from, 5–6
Chemical pollution, 27
Circulation, in cold, 12
Cirrocumuli clouds, 9
Cirrostratus clouds, 9
Cirrus clouds, 9
Clothing, 4, 7, 14, 17
    benefits of light-colored, 14
Clouds, in weather forecasting, 7–9
Clover, 34
Cold hazards, 12–13

Compass, 4, 6, 7, 45–47, 55
Cooking, 39
Cumulonimbus clouds, 7–9
Cumulus clouds, 7
Current, river, 16–17

Dandelions, 34
Department of Energy, Mines and Resources (Canada), 6
Desert, 13, 30
Dew, 9, 28
Directional aids, 42–48

Emergencies, 10–22
Equipment, 6–7, 56–57
Evergreen trees, 9
Exposure, effects of, 11–12

Ferns, 36
Fire, 23–25
    building of, 24–25
    as signal, 50
    use in sterilizing water, 25–28
First-aid kit, 6, 57
Fish, 37–38
Fishing gear, 56
Flashlight, 6, 7, 56
Food, 13–14, 33–39
    cooking methods, 39
    determining edible plants, 33–37
    eating animals, 37–38
    edible insects, 37
Frogs, 38
Frost, 9
Frostbite, 12–13

Getting lost. See Lost, being
Glasses, eye, 55
    used to make fire, 24
Gooseberries, 36, 37
Grasshoppers, 37

Hail, 9
Heat hazards, 13–14
Hexamine (combustible tablets), 25
Hiking, 3, 4
Hinged mirror compass, 45, 47
Hypothermia, 11–12

Ice, falling through, 17
Insects, 15–16
    edible, 37
Iodine, 15, 16

Knives, 6, 7, 17, 56

Landmarks, 41, 45
Lensatic compass, 45–47
Lichens, 36
Lightning, 9
Little Dipper, 44
Liquor, 32
Lost, being, and reorientation, 40–48

Magnetic north, 45–47
Maps, 4, 6, 41
Matches, 4, 6, 7, 23–24, 55
Mirrors, 6, 51–53
Mites, 15
Morale, 53
Mosquitoes, 16
Mushrooms, 33–34

Needle and thread, 57
Nimbostratus clouds, 9
North, finding, 44, 45–47
Nuts, 34–36

Nylon cord, 6

Organic pollution, 27
Outdoor survival
    coping with emergencies, 10–22
    energy conservation, 47–48
    equipment, 6–7, 56–57
    getting lost and finding one's way, 40–48
    maintaining morale, 53
    planning ahead, 5–7
    signaling, 49–53

Panic, 10–11
Pine tree, as shelter, 9
Plants
    edible, 33–37
    poisonous, 18, 33–36
Plastic, for lightweight kits, 55
Poison ivy, 18
Poison oak, 18
Poison sumac, 18
Polaris, 44
Polestar, 44
Pollution, of water, 27–28

Quicksand, 18

Rain, 7–9

Salt, 30–32
Seawater, 30–32
Seaweed, 36
Shellfish, 38
Shock, 11
Shoes, 4, 21
Sidestroke, 17
Signaling, 49–53
Signaling mirror, 51–53
Space blanket, 6, 7
Spotted fever vaccine, 16

Snakebite kit, 6, 18, 56
Snakebites, 18–21
Snow, 12–13, 14–15
Snowblindness, 21–22
Soap, 56
S-O-S, signaling, 50–51
Stars, as directional aids, 44
Sun, as directional aid, 43–44, 51
Sunburn, 7, 14
Sunglasses, 7, 22
Swimming
    in fast current, 16–17
    in quicksand, 18
Symbols, for S-O-S, 50–51

Tetanus booster shot, 7
Thermometer, 9
Thread, 57
Ticks, 15–16
Tourist offices, 5–6
Tourniquet, 21

Tree bark, edible, 36
Trout, 37

U.S. Geological Survey, 6

Water, 13, 25–32, 33
    collected from air, 28
    in desert, 28–30
    pollution of, 27–28
    purification tablets, 16, 27–28
    at sea, 30–32
    substitutes for, 32
Water flask, 7
Water-purifying tablets, 6, 27–28, 56
Weather, 4, 7–9, 12
    cold hazards, 12–13
    heat hazards, 13–14
Whistle, 51, 56
Winds, 9
Wire, 56
Wolves, 14

About the Author

Born in London, England, Charles Platt has been living in New York City for the past six years. The author is a free-lance writer and editorial consultant with varied interests. He is the author of several science fiction novels for young readers and has also written on craft and decorating topics. Though an avid table tennis enthusiast when confined to the city, his favorite leisure activity is backpacking—preferably in the Rocky Mountains.